YOUR DREAMS MATTER!

YOUR DREAMS MATTER!

7 Things Your Dreams Need from You

Herbert Fenner

To order additional copies of this book, contact:
Xlibris
844-714-8691
www.Xlibris.com
Orders@Xlibris.com
827724

CONTENTS

It is with extreme joy as well as sadness that I dedicate this book to my friend and brother Danta "Fat Tater" Barksdale, also known as "the man with the big voice." Every chance we got to talk, we discussed our dreams and how we were going to make our dreams a reality. You inspired me so much through your hard work, commitment, and dedication to making our streets safe. Your life spoke for you, and your message of love and hope continues to reverberate throughout the world. I wish you were here to celebrate this accomplishment, and I know that you would be proud of me as I am of you. While you rest in heaven, I will continue make a difference, doing something that makes a difference with people like yourself who is making a difference. Until we meet again, my friend. You are truly missed but will never be forgotten. RIP, Tater.

ACKNOWLEDGMENTS

Heartfelt gratitude to some meaningful people in my life:

My mother Celestina Fenner, my rock who continues to believe in me and covers me with powerful, heartfelt prayer.

My wife Yvette Fenner, who encourages me and continues to support my vision to add value to the world. I love you, and I don't know where I would be without you and the love that you have for me. Thank you, babe, for all that you do to make me the man that I am.

My friend and brother from another mother Louis L. Reed, who had made it known that he would hold me *responsible* for completing this book. We did it, sir, and I want to thank you for being there every step of the way.

You are an amazing friend, brother, and leader. Thanks for believing in me and adding value to this book.

My Master Mind group, *The 15 Invaluable Laws of Growth*, for allowing me to pour into you what my mentor Dr. John C. Maxwell has poured into me. I have seen your growth, and I'm honored to have coached such an amazing group. Special thanks to Angela Harrison, Jacque Franklin, and Karen Malone. Remember that *growth is intentional*.

My brother Terry Fenner, who constantly reminds me that I have unlimited potential and that I have to keep grinding until I win.

I express gratitude to all those who support me and my message: "It's your story, and you can rewrite it if you want to."

COMMITMENT

The willingness to give your time and energy to something that you believe or a promise or firm decision to do something

If you are reading the pages from this book, it can only mean one thing, and that is I was committed. I had a willingness to give my time and energy to something that I believe in. And that something for me is my dreams. My dreams consist of adding value to people while at the same time making myself more valuable.

And what better way to do both than by writing a book on seven things that your dreams need from you? If you notice, I said "need" and not "want" from you because wants are not a necessity. Things that I want is not something that

I must have. But things that I need is necessary if I am going to get the desired results.

The moment I decided that I was going to write this book, I reached out to a close friend whom I respect in the field of leadership, and I told him that I needed him to hold me accountable for completing this book. But his response was I need to hold you responsible for writing this book.

I must admit it took me twenty-four hours to process what he had said. My friend Louis L. Reed has a way with words and had a way of making you think deeper. Louis understood the difference in being accountable and being held responsible. Being held accountable is something that I wanted for me, but being responsible is something that my dreams needed to keep it from being deferred.

Dreams are gifts from God, which begins as a seed planted in your mind. And like any other seed, your dreams require nurturing if it is going to grow and produce fruit. Sad to say many of my dreams had been deferred and some even died because neglect and being irresponsible.

Irresponsibility is a dream killer to say the least. My wife understands the importance of being responsible when it comes to the growth and success of our marriage and relationship. She would often remind me that *I have to water her.* In other words, to keep my marriage from dying, it was my responsibility to attend to it. It was my responsibility to give our marriage what it needed for it to grow.

And one of the things my marriage, as well as my dreams, needed is my commitment. If you want your dreams to live and not die, it is going to need your commitment. If you want your dreams to move beyond just a thought in your head to becoming a reality in your life, it is going to need your commitment.

There must be a *willingness to give your time and energy to something you believe in*, and that is your dreams. For most of my life, I had the motivation to start something but lacked the commitment to keep going. And as a result, the attic of my mind is filled with dreams that have been deferred and often forgotten about. If I were to take some time to clean out the attic in my mind, I would find books that I started to write but never completed. I would find business ideas that have collected dust because of neglect. I would find premature and stillborn dreams that no one ever knew existed because of neglect and irresponsibility.

What about you? What will we find in the attic of your mind that is collecting dust? Will we find books you never published? Will we find great ideas and inventions that have been left to die because of neglect? Will we find the cure for a disease that has yet to be discovered or a business plan that could potentially save millions of people only if they knew it existed?

The tragedy in neglecting a dream is in the lives of those who could be affected by it. And to have a cure and not share it is criminal to say the least. Every day we are exposed to people's dreams that have made its way to our medical cabinets, our refrigerators, our closets, our communities, our driveways, and our schools. It is the dreams of our favorite comedians, such as Kevin Hart, Martin Lawrence,

Eddie Murphy, that make us laugh and escape our pain. It is the dreams of our inventors, such as George Washington Carver, Madam C. J. Walker, George Crum, that allow us to enjoy life and keep the bottom of our feet from scraping the ground. It is the dreams of our educators that challenge us to be our best selves.

The world that we live in and often enjoy comes at a cost. And that cost, my friend, is commitment. For it has been said by Bishop T. D. Jakes, a man I highly respect, that "without commitment, nothing happens." Without commitment, the world, as we know it, will not exist. So my question for you is, are you committed to giving your dreams what it needs for your dreams to survive? Are you committed to watering your dreams so your dreams can grow? Because if you are not committed, *nothing is going to happen.*

Pat Riley once said, "There are only two options regarding commitment: You're either in or you're out. There's no such thing as life in-between."

I remember hearing this story about this general who decided that he was going to conquer this island and take it over. The general gathered his small army of about twenty soldiers, and they set sail to conquer the island. As the general and his army approached the shores of the island, they were met with opposition. The chants of what appeared to be hundreds of armed and courageous men thundered and shook the very ground of the island. The thunder grew louder as the armed and courageous men drew closer to the general and his small army of about twenty men. But what happened next stopped the army of courageous men in their tracks, causing them to lay down their weapons and surrender. The islanders watched with fear and awe as the general lit a torch and set the boats he and his men had traveled in on fire. Before setting sail to conquer the island, the general had a pep talk with his men, and the conversation went something like this: "We are going to conquer this island, or we will die trying. But retreat is not an option."

For the general and his men, there was no in-between. They were committed, even if it meant death. When it comes to your dreams and making your dreams a reality, it is either you are in or you are out. There is no in-between. Retreat and aborting your dreams should never be an option. And to keep to your commitment, there may be some things that you need to burn that can serve as a bridge to take you in the opposite direction of where you should be going.

There are some negative people in your life whom you may have to cut ties with if you are going to fulfill your dreams. There are some bad habits and addictions that need to be eliminated for your dreams to stand a chance of surviving.

Commitment requires sacrifice. Commitment requires you to make choices for you to make changes. The general understood that you cannot conquer what you are not committed to.

Vince Lombardi was correct when he stated, "Most

people fail not because of a lack of desire but because of a lack of commitment." I found out, through aborting my dreams, that desire is not enough to achieve anything worthwhile.

Every year since I can remember, myself, along with thousands of others, make New Year's resolutions, only to end the year disappointed and discouraged. We had the desire to lose weight and join the gym. We had the desire to save some money and start our own business. We had the desire to work on ourselves and become better husbands, wives, parents, and human beings. But without commitment, we are left disappointed and discouraged. Without commitment, the music stops, and the celebration party is once again put on hold.

If you believe in your dreams like I know you do, it is time to be committed to them. It is time to nurture your dreams and spend some time cultivating them. Commitment means *staying loyal to what you said you were going to do long after the mood you said it in has left you.*"

When all the motivation is gone, your commitment must remain. It has been said, "To thine own self be true." I take this to mean when it comes to your dreams, which is a part of you and resides within you, you must be committed. The birth of our dreams is our responsibility.

My seven-year-old daughter, after waking up, stumbles to find me in my study and, with sleep still in her eyes, says, "Daddy, I'm hungry." She does not take it upon herself to try to cook for herself because my daughter understands that feeding her, providing for her, and protecting her is my responsibility. It is a responsibility that I cannot ignore, regardless of how I may be feeling or what I may be doing. Feeding my daughter is something that I am committed to. Providing for my daughter is something that I am committed to. And for me to neglect this responsibility will have serious consequences.

Your dreams cannot feed itself, and if you do not feed your dreams, it will wither and eventually die. No more aborting your dreams. No more excuses for not being committed to that seed that was planted in your mind. Every day you must check in on your dreams. It is like being a parent. When you have a new baby, you do not just put your baby in a crib and leave your baby to care for itself. You check in on your baby every so often because you care about your baby and you know that your baby cannot care for itself. Commitment is the *little choices every day that lead to the final results we are striving for.* Every day look to see if you are giving your dreams the attention it needs. Every day take some time to listen to your dreams.

Our dreams speak, and you will only hear it if you are listening. Your dreams will tell you what it needs, and if you do not know, we will cover it in this book. But the first thing your dreams need is your commitment because *without commitment, nothing happens.* Be committed to making your dreams a reality. Clean the attic of your mind out, and bring your dreams back to life. Your dreams dies only if you allow it to die.

It was my dream to write a self-help book and a book on

leadership. But I lost focus and neglected my responsibility. I began to doubt my ability to write such a book. And like so many other dreams I had, I released it to the attic of my mind. But this one, this dream, I refused to let it die. I refused to allow nothing to happen for me because I lacked commitment. I refused to get the same results of a heart filled with regret and another dream deferred.

It has been said that if you want something different, then you have to do something different. I wanted something different, and I know that you want something different also. I wanted to make my dreams a reality. I wanted to experience the joy of a mother after she has carried a child in her womb for nine long months then pushes out of her that dream that was inside of her. I wanted to birth forth those ideas that were inside of me. I felt it, but now I needed to see it. I needed for the world to see my dreams and be blessed by it. I needed the world to know that my dreams exist.

In 2016, I launched Invisible Ink Leadership

Development. Starting a business that would serve as a platform to add value to people and their business was one of my dreams, a dream that was no longer deferred. I carried Invisible Ink inside of me for ten years before I gave birth to it. I refused to let this dream die. So I continued to push. I continued to stay committed. I nurtured my dream until it was time for my dream to be birthed. I did something different, and I received something different. I got the chance to see what I had been feeling inside me for over ten years. I got the chance to see my dream manifest itself in organizations, such as T-Mobile, public schools, housing developments, churches, youth organizations, colleges, and more.

I got the chance to add value to thousands of people via social media because I did not allow Invisible Ink to die. Do not allow your dreams of starting your own business to die. Do not allow your dreams of buying a home and taking care of your family to die. Somebody needs to read that book that is inside of you. Somebody needs to hear about the ideas that are going to save the lives of our youth. Somebody is licking their lips, waiting for the new recipe to launch.

If you want something different tomorrow, then do something different today. Make the commitment to give your dream the time and energy it needs. Take some time to go into the attic of your mind and set the captive free. Allow the world to know that your dreams exist and your dreams matter. Allow the world to know that you are committed to making your dreams a reality and aborting your dreams is not an option. And remember and never forget that *without commitment, nothing happens.*

Commitment is the difference between a starter and a finisher. Everyone starts, but it is only those who are committed finish. If you are going to stay committed, it is important that you keep the end in mind. Think about how you feel when you keep your commitment. Every time I complete something that I am committed to, my confidence toward the next goal increases. What is one thing you have started that you would like to finish? This is your time to separate yourself from the starters and become a finisher.

Finishers are willing to stay committed until the task is completed. Finishers see their dreams through and make no excuses about why they cannot but give themselves reasons why they can. When I started writing this book, I knew that I had to finish it, and it was my commitment that was going to see it through. If I fail to finish this project, then I will have little to no confidence going into the next project.

Being confronted with many obstacles and opposition, like depression and an anxiety disorder, my commitment was my driving force. There were days when I could not focus and had to step away from writing because of anxiety. There were days when I wanted to just give up, but I could not because not only was I committed, but I was also responsible for finishing what I started.

You have a responsibility to push past the obstacles and the self-doubt. You have a responsibility to fight for your dreams. Everyone gets knocked down, but those who are committed gets back up. It is time to get back up, my friend, and finish what you started. It is time to get back into the race. This race is not over until you win. Do not start another project until you finish the ones that you have neglected. Do not take another class until you complete the class you dropped. Repeat these words: "Today I will make a commitment to finish what I started." And with those words as your driving force, I will see you at the finish line.

Vision

If you can dream it, you can do it. —Walt Disney

The company I started in 2016 started as a thought seed in my mind while I was in an obscure place—a federal prison. It was 2005, and I had four years to serve on a prison sentence of seventeen years. I was at work in a prison factory, working as a payroll accountant. This job was a big deal for me, especially considering that I had dropped out of high school and had to settle for a GED.

But with some encouragement and a burning desire to do better for myself, I decided to go back to school. After obtaining my GED, I decided to enroll in college to get my degree in business management. At this point in my life, I was still uncertain about the direction I wanted to go in. Going to school taught me how to study and focus. Going to school taught me how to think and reason. Going to school gave me structure and meaning, and I am saying "school" and not "college" because I believe any learning institution can help you become a better thinker and teach you the importance of responsibility.

I felt good carrying my books and telling people that I was in college. I felt good getting good grades after getting a F in the lessons of life. I was on my way, I thought, but with deeper reflection, I really did not have a clue about where I was going. Once again, I was following the crowd. At the time, going to school for business management was the thing to do, so I did it.

For over ten years, I made sure the brothers received their wages every month with accuracy because I understood that in prison, every penny counts because that is all you were getting paid literally. I was good at what I did as a payroll accountant, but that was not my passion. My passion was connecting with people and helping people have hope and a better life. I wanted to be around people and influence them. God knew my passion, and out of my passion, I discovered my purpose.

I remember sitting at my desk at work, looking out of a window that only looked onto the prison grounds. My body was there, but my mind had wandered off. Instantly, I found myself walking around a mall. Without any destination, I just walked around, enjoying the freedom and the scenery. I then noticed this long line that led to a bookstore. I have never seen anything like this before. Over the years, I had become an avid reader and had a love for books. I was curious and excited, so I decided to ask what was going on. I stepped into the back of the line and asked those in front of me why the line was so long. With excitement, all I heard was "It's here, it's finally here!"

Well, that did not tell me much, so I probed further. "What's here?"

"What we all been waiting for" was the response I got. Still not making sense of what everyone was waiting for, I just decided to wait and see. After patiently waiting, I finally reached the cashier. And with excitement, I handed the cashier my money, and in return, she handed me a book that was resting inside of a beautiful box. I guess presentation does matter because I was sold on the box.

Curious to find out what all the excitement was about, I rushed to the parking lot and started opening the box. Removing the book with haste, I opened the book and began flipping through the pages. To my surprise, as well as disappointment, all the pages were blank. Did I just wait all that time for a bad copy of the book? Disappointed but still curious about the book, I decided to exchange it. When I approached the cashier, before I could open my mouth to say anything, I noticed a sign that hung over the cashier head that I did not notice the first time. The sign read in bold black letters, "THE BOOK WITH THE INVISIBLE INK."

With my head held down, I gripped the book tightly and walked away. As I was walking away, I looked at the line. There were people from all different nationalities.

This line represented the real united nations; it represented humanity. But why were all these people here is what I wanted to know. Why are they waiting for a book with blank pages? With no understanding, I asked God what this meant, and this is the revelation I received: All the people represented all of humanity, and the book with the invisible ink allowed them to rewrite their story. The book with the invisible ink allowed them to change characters and switch rolls. The book with the invisible ink allowed them to change the narrative in their story. The more God revealed, the more excited I got.

This was it, I said to myself. This was the vision that showed me my purpose. God allowed for me to see it, and now that I saw my purpose, I had to make a commitment to be it. I had never experienced anything like this before. I wanted to live in the moment. But I could not. God gave me the vision, and it was now my job to make it a reality. It was my time to rewrite my story. I began to see myself different. I was changing characters. I was switching roles.

It has been said, if I see you as you are, you'll remain as you are, but if I see you as you could be, I help you become as you should be.

I was no longer just an inmate with a number. I was no longer a statistic or an accident waiting to happen. I was changing characters and switching roles. I started seeing myself helping people and speaking in front of thousands of people. I saw myself counseling people and motivating people. I saw myself writing books and adding value to people.

Life, as I once knew it, was changing simply because I had the power to change it. I was no longer seeing my life as it was but as it could be. How do you see yourself? This is an especially important question that is worth looking at because how you see yourself will determine how you treat yourself. If you see yourself as unfit or as a Section 8, you will treat yourself that way. If you see yourself as being unworthy of happiness and success, you will treat yourself that way. If you see yourself as having a disability and a dark cloud hanging over your head, you will treat yourself that way. So if things in your life, as well as mine, are going to change, then you and I will have to change it.

I wanted to change the narrative of my life story. I wanted to switch roles to become the helper and not the helpless. I wanted to be the hero and not the victim. I wanted to be the prodigal son who once was lost but now has been found, who once was dead but is alive again. And for that to happen, I had to change my thinking.

James Allen wrote a life-changing book, *As a Man Thinks*, that underlines the importance of having the right thinking. We cannot separate our thinking from who we are. We are what we think. If you think you cannot, then you will not. Your dreams need your vision.

Your vision allows you to see and feel what you are capable of. Anything that you can see within reason, you can become. Since I had been out of prison, I have been able to reach thousands of people through Invisible Ink, my books, speaking, trainings, social media, work, and ministry. And I am just getting started.

What are you afraid of? Are you afraid to fail? What if I told you that there is only one way to fail and that is not by trying at all? Everything else is a plus. You stepped out on what you said you believed in to make it a reality. I want to give the world something it could touch and build a connection with, and that is an environment conducive for growth and development, a place where people who had been hurt, rejected, and counted out can bounce back and rewrite their story.

I know I am not there yet, but I am moving in the direction of achieving this goal and dream. When the vision came to me, I was in prison. So where do you think I started at? Yes, in prison. You must begin where you are at, wherever that may be. If you know anyone who has ever achieved their dreams, for them to get to where they are at, they had to begin where they were. Where you begin is not as important as where you end. Your beginning is part of the journey, a critical part because it is important that you start now. Yes, begin your journey where you are at, with what you have.

While in prison, I started working on my craft. I was teaching Bible studies and adult continuance education classes. Every time I opened my mouth, I was perfecting my craft as a speaker. I began where I was, and through commitment and encouragement, I started *making a difference, doing something that makes a difference with people who are making a difference at a time that makes a difference.* I began where I was, with what I had.

People oftentimes ask me, after they hear me speak, where I learned to speak like that. "I learned in prison" is always my response. I practiced my talent on my job. What you do not use you will lose. I must stay ready for bigger opportunities. It has been said, it's better to be ready for opportunities and not have one than to have opportunities and not be ready. Use your job as a place to nurture your talents and gifts. There is only one way to get good at something, and no, it is not by watching but by doing.

Volunteer so you can get yourself out there. Take your dreams for a test drive. See how people will respond to your service. Give away something for free. Who does not like free? Your dreams need your vision. Give it character and bring your dreams to life. Start baking, if you like to bake, and give them away. Get out of the house so the world can know you exist. Whatever your dreams need you to do, do it now. Procrastination is a dream killer. Thomas Edison says, "Vision without execution is hallucination."

This is your moment, your season. It is time to become your best self. It is time to change the narrative in your story. How do you see yourself? I need you to see yourself, not where you are at, but where you are trying to go. See yourself smiling again. See yourself with your own business and traveling. See yourself not having to struggle to pay your bills. See yourself free from addictions that has caused you to abort your dreams.

See it, then follow the road that will take you there. All around you lies opportunities to show the world what you can do to make it better. And where there is no path, you create one. Going back to old ways of thinking and living is not an option. Going back into a troubled relationship is not an option. Dropping out of school is not an option. Resist by all means. Resist the urge to quit. Resist the urge to do anything that will not bring you closer to fulfilling your dreams. Resist the negative thoughts in your head that are telling you that you cannot do it.

You can do it, and you must believe that you can. Every day I listen to positive affirmations. I listen to motivational speeches to combat the negative self-talk that goes on in my head. Positive motivation will get you going, but commitment will keep you growing. It is time to be committed to the execution of your vision. No more hallucination. It is time to silence your fear of failure. And the way you do this is not by what you say but by what you do. Your actions should override any negative thoughts you may have. Feel the fear, embrace it, and then do it anyway.

There is a song that says, "Let my life speak for me." These words are true. The life that you live will speak for you. The choices that you make will speak for you. Our actions always speak louder than our words. Through our actions, we tell the world what we believe and stand for. If the life you are living is not saying what you want it to say, then change your life. And keep changing your life until your life is saying what you want it to say. I want my life to speak life and not death. My life is a message of hope. My life encourages people to know that there is a God, a life that was full of darkness and despair but is now full of life and light.

The dark days of my life did not define me, they did not kill me, but the dark days of depression, anxiety, and struggle only made me stronger. Like many of you, I have been through hell, but I learned early on in life that when you are going through hell, do not stop, keep going. Your dreams need you to keep going. You cannot afford to stop or quit. *For the race is not given to the swift nor the strong but to those who endures until the end.* Your speed does not matter, neither does your strength, when it comes to achieving your dreams and goals. The only thing that matters is your willingness to finish what God started in your mind. Will you, my friend, keep going?

Writing this book brought me joy. I started out strong. I felt encouraged and motivated. I was excited on this journey, but for me to share my excitement with the world, I must keep going. Do not deprive the world of your goods and services. We need your life to speak for you. Let your light shine in a world that is full of darkness. Let the world see and feel what you have been seeing and feeling through your vision. Bring us in on the experience. Give us a sample of what is to come. Let the world know that it is finally here, that what we have all been waiting for is finally here.

We have been waiting for you long enough. Now it is time to present to the world your best self, your creative ideas. Let us sample your best recipe. Let us hear those jokes you have been working on and those songs you have been practicing. Let us model that business idea that is going to bring comfort to hurting parents who lost their children. Tell us what we can do to save our youth from violence and gangs. The world needs to hear from you because from where I am standing, those things have yet to be figured out. For the problems in the world are plentiful, but the solutions are few.

We have more problems than solutions. This world needs answers; our communities need answers, our children need answers, and your vision needs to connect with the problems because your vision carries the answers. Remember, *if you can dream it, you can do it*. You can rewrite your story because I did. You can change characters because I did. You can make a difference, and you will make a difference, because I did. Give your dreams what it needs, and in return, your dreams will give you what you need. Your dreams will give you purpose. Your dreams will give your life meaning. Your dreams will take you places that you will never be able to travel without it. Your dreams need your vision, and *without vision, people perish.*

Your vision is going to help someone. Your vision is going to give someone a better quality of life. There is no need for the people to perish. There is no need for our youth to be murdered and our elderly to be mistreated. There is no need for our mothers, fathers, brothers, and sisters to die from drug overdose. There is no need for people to lose hope to the point of taking their own lives. These things can change, and all it takes is *the execution of our vision.* All it takes is for us to believe in our vision. Your life is speaking for you, and the world is waiting to see what it is that you have to say.

Faith

Taking the first step even when you
don't see the whole staircase

I remember one evening while in prison, I was sitting
on the edge of my bed, reading. My roommate was lying
down, playing possum. I never met anyone like him before.
His name was Cowboy, at least that is what we called
him. Cowboy was sixty years old and was only serving a
one-year sentence. Cowboy was married to some younger
woman, and he was about to have his first child. When
they say age is nothing but a number, Cowboy lived by
that motto. Cowboy used to do one-handed push-ups and
pull-ups. Cowboy was not only in great shape physically
but also mentally. Cowboy was full of wisdom, and it was

his wisdom that gave me a clear picture of what it means to have faith.

While in prison, God always placed me in a position to learn something. When I say that God will never leave you nor forsake you, I am a living witness to this truth. It's true when they say, "When the student is ready, the master will appear."

Leaping up from his bed, as if he had a bad dream, Cowboy sat on the edge of the bed and looked at me with this stern look on his face. I could tell Cowboy was in deep thought, and whatever he had on his mind captured his full attention.

To keep from disturbing his thought process, I did not say a word. I just kept reading my book. Moments later, Cowboy looked up at me again and said, "If this room started to fill up with water, how would you get out of here?"

Instantly, Cowboy had my full attention. I did not know where Cowboy was going with this, but I was curious to find out. Repeating himself, Cowboy said, "If this room starts to fill up with water, how will you get out of here?"

I started looking around the room for a way out. The problem I was having was, for one, the door to the room was locked from the outside. The doors were made of steel, and no matter what you did to it, that steel door was not going to budge. I than started looking at the window. The window did not open, and if it did, the window was so narrow, there was no way anyone could squeeze through it. So going out through the door or window was not an option. I then started looking for other ways to escape a room that was flooding with water. But as far as I could see, there was no way out. There was no way for me to escape a room flooding with water.

Seeing that I had given up my search, Cowboy looked at my helpless self and said, "Your faith—your faith is going to get you out of here."

Grasping the Bible that I was reading; I knew that God had used Cowboy to teach me a valuable lesson that day.

This was a lesson that I felt compelled to share with you because this lesson about faith is one of, if not the most important lesson I learned in my life.

If I were going to live my dreams, I needed to have faith. If you are going to live out your dreams, then you must also have faith. Your dreams begin as a small seed in your mind. But how do you get your dreams to grow? How do you take something that is planted inside of you to manifest itself outside of you? How do you take an impossible situation and make it possible? The answer is your faith. Your need for faith to make your dreams come true is an indication that your dreams are bigger than you and to make it grow is going to require that you trust in someone that is bigger than you.

Cowboy was teaching me that just because I did not know how to escape a prison cell filling up with water did not mean that there was not a way out. It just meant that I needed help to do what I could not do by myself. There will be doors closed that you cannot open by yourself. You will not know the right people or have the money to launch your ideas. Doing these critical moments, you must rely on your faith. And how do you rely on your faith? You rely on your faith by not giving in to your fear. You rely on your faith by moving forward despite of.

Despite of how things may look, you must continue to move forward. Despite of your lack of resources, you must continue to move forward. Despite of not feeling adequate or worthy of your dreams, you must continue to move forward. Faith is moving forward until you cannot go any further in and of your own strength.

The children of Israel were led out of Egypt by a man who thought of himself as being inadequate. Moses did not believe he was the man for the job. Moses had a disability and felt that his disability would excuse him from his life purpose. Are you allowing your disability to paralyze you and keep you from living your dreams? Did you know that fear was a disability? Moses told God that he had a speech problem and would never be able to represent God's people before the pharaoh. Moses thought he escaped his responsibility, but what Moses failed to realize was that God always makes a way. Moses said, "I have a problem," and God told Moses, in other words however, "That's good, Moses, because I am the solution to your problem."

Moses looked up and saw the solution to his problem walking toward him. God told Moses, "I understand that you have a speech problem, so I sent your brother Aaron to be your spokesman."

Faith is believing and trusting that God is going to give you everything you need to accomplish your mission and fulfill your dreams. So if you have a disability or an excuse for not following your dream, I need you, my friend, to look up. Because God is going to send you the help you need. God will send you the resources you need.

When Moses and the children of Israel crossed the Red Sea, they complained to Moses because they had another problem: They did not have food or the means to get any food. Moses then took the complaint to God, and God said to Moses, "Look up." When Moses looked up, God began to send him manna, food from heaven.

The point I am making is we must continue to look out and look up. And when I say "look up," I am not talking about standing still and gazing into outer space. That is daydreaming. Looking up means to show signs of improving. And the only way my life will improve is when I improve. Faith without works is dead. It does not matter how much faith I have in my marriage, if I do not water my marriage, it is going to die. If you do not water your dreams, your dreams will die. If you do not water your potential, your potential is going to die. Do not allow your dreams to die, my friend. Hold on to your faith. Continue to work on yourself even if there is not an opportunity visible. It has been said, it is better to be ready for an opportunity and not have one than have an opportunity and not be ready. Your faith is needed for you to move some mountains that will try to get in your way and keep you from fulfilling your dreams.

Mountains like fear and doubt will try to stop you. Mountains like low self-esteem and feelings of unworthiness will try to stop you. Whatever your mountains may be, they are there to stop you from living your dream. One of my mountains is anxiety and depression. And as I was writing this chapter, my mountain showed up. My mind was under attack. For two weeks, I could not write. I did not understand where this attack was coming from because it struck me without warning. But I knew that this sudden attack of anxiety and depression had a purpose, and that purpose was to stop me from reaching my goals. Its purpose was to keep me from writing this book.

But I was determined to finish what I started, so I called on my family and friends. I needed the prayers of the righteous that avails much. I shared with family and friends what I was going through, knowing that some would not understand, but I took the risk, a risk that paid off because I had faith. Faith moves mountains, but that faith cannot just be in yourself. Our faith must involve other people because two strong cords are not easily broken. On this journey called life, we have to get others involved because no one can succeed alone. Anxiety and depression had invaded my space, and it was not a pleasant experience. But I got through it because I looked up. I looked toward God and others to draw strength from.

Apart from God, who are you looking toward to draw strength from? Do not make the mistake of thinking that you do not need anyone. Do not make the mistake of thinking that your problems are not that big and you can handle them alone. Get other people involved and allow them to hold you up during your challenging and difficult times. And if you have not experienced any yet, just keep pursuing your dreams, and I guarantee that you will.

No one is exempt from the trials and frustrations of life, especially when you are working on your goals and dreams. As men and women of faith, we are told, "Think is not strange concerning the fiery trials which is to try you, as though some strange thing happened to you," 1 Peter 4:12.

In other words, do not be surprised when your faith is being tested. Do not be surprised when your dreams are being challenged with fear and doubt. Opposition is not only to be expected, but it is also to be embraced. Opposition is not your enemy; it is your opportunity. Opposition is your opportunity to utilize it to grow in your faith. Opposition is your opportunity to see how much you have grown and how much more you need to grow. The challenges you face are going to reveal and build your character.

The apostle Peter learned this valuable lesson during a critical time in his ministry. Peter had been walking alongside Jesus for three years. Peter had walked on water, cast out demons, and performed miracles. Peter felt like he had arrived spiritually, but Jesus knew otherwise. Jesus informed his disciples that his time had come for him to be betrayed and taken captive. And Peter responded with spiritual pride. Peter insisted that he was going to not allow this to happen to Jesus and that he would ride and die with

Jesus. But Peter forgot an important lesson, and that lesson is that *pride comes before a fall.*

Peter had good intentions, but how many of you know that good intentions never show up? When it came time for Peter to put his money where his mouth was, Peter did not show up. Peter, not once but on three different occasions, denied his association with Jesus. This test for Peter revealed something in Peter. It revealed that he was not as committed as he wanted others to believe. His pride brought about his fall.

What are your challenges and struggles revealing about you? Has opposition and challenges caused you to deny your dreams? Have you given up because of challenges and setbacks? How committed are you? And trust me when I say *your actions will speak louder than your words.*

I have many unfinished projects simply because I was not as committed as I wanted to believe I was. And the trials of life exposed me for my lack of commitment. But what do we do when we are exposed? What do we do when we come to realize that we are not where we expect to be at this phase of our life? You do what Peter did—you recover, and you bounce back. But by no means do you quit.

We learn from our failures and shortcomings. We grow, and we move on. Like Peter, you will be tested again. You will have another opportunity to show that you are committed to your dreams. But until that time comes, take this time to build on areas of weakness. Take this time to examine yourself and remember, "To thine own self be true." Do not compare yourself to other people, and do not try to compete with others. Focus on being the best you that you can be. Trust the process, and allow your faith to grow.

Are your dreams worth fighting for? They should be, so get back in the fight and start swinging. Get back in the gym and start swinging. Get back in the ministry and start swinging. Whatever your dreams may be, it is time to bounce back and start swinging. The only chance you will have of hitting a home run is by swinging the bat. Swing your faith, and if you keep swinging, you will connect to your dreams, and as the saying goes, *the rest will be history.*

When I was faced with the anxiety and depression, I was determined to get back up swinging. I was determined to not give up on my dreams. Your dreams need you to keep swinging. Remember, *faith is taking the first step even when you don't see the whole staircase.* Do not worry about completing the book you are assigned to write, just get the first word down, and that word will become a sentence, and that sentence will become a chapter, and that chapter will become a book. Do not worry about where you will get the money from, just use your gifts to add value to people, and your gifts will make room for you. When you are faced with the question of how you will do it, and it seems impossible, your answer should be "my faith."

GROWTH

We cannot become what we want by remaining what we are. —Max Depree

Leadership guru Dr. John C. Maxwell, one of my mentors, wrote a book titled *The 15 Invaluable Laws of Growth*. This book has been one of my personal growth tools. And it was in this book that I discovered the importance of having a growth plan.

Like many of you, I knew what it meant to have goals and the importance of setting goals. But I had not a clue of what a personal growth plan was, neither its importance. I had assumed that if I set goals and reach my goals, then that was an indication of growth. But I soon learned that

I was wrong in my assumption, and if I was truly going to grow, my thinking had to change.

Today, in my practice as a leader, coach, pastor, and mentor, I find myself challenging other people's assumptions by challenging them to develop a personal growth plan. And now that I have your attention, I would also like to challenge your assumption in hopes that I can help you grow and, as a result, live your dreams.

I remember working as a behavior specialist in the Baltimore public school system. Report cards had just come out, and I recall having a conversation with a student who had been known for having behavioral issues. This student hardly went to class, and when he decided to go, he was often removed for disrupting the class. So I was surprised to hear him say that he had passed, and he was extremely excited as well as shocked. On the other hand, I was disappointed, not in the student but in the system that allowed such a thing. After having a conversation with the school administrator, I was told the student could pass and move forward because the school did not have enough teachers to teach them, and the students couldn't be held responsible.

Still disappointed, I left the administrator's office and went to visit the student. Looking the student in his eyes, I asked him, "What was your goal?" and the student said his goal was to pass. I then asked the student, "Did you accomplish your goal?" With a smile on his face, he said yes. My next question to the student was, "What did you learn?" As I expected, there was silence because I knew that the student had not learned anything. The student accomplished his goal, but there was no growth because he did not learn anything.

Just because you reach your goal does not guarantee growth. But if you shift your mind to growth, you are guaranteed to reach your goal. This shift in thinking keeps me on my toes because goals have a date, but growth is continuous. I have met many professional people who have degrees but have become ineffective and partly because they do not have a growth mindset. For your dreams to become a reality, you must keep growing, you must keep learning.

Joining the John C. Maxwell Team gave me the platform to keep growing. This organization allowed me to develop a personal growth plan. *The 15 Invaluable Laws of Growth* is a book that I would strongly recommend if you are serious about your dreams and living to your full potential. I would like to discuss with you some of the things I learned from this book and how it has helped me.

The first law John teaches is the Law of Intentionality, and it says, "Growth doesn't just happen." In other words, your growth on all levels must be deliberate. If I were to ask you, when you examine your life, would you agree that there is room in your life to grow? When you look at your health, is there room in your health to get better? When you look at your career, is there room to get better? When you look at your faith, is there room to get better? If we are honest, the answer is yes, yes, yes, and yes. Because there is always room to grow, there is always room to get better.

I love how Max Depree put it: "We cannot become what we want by remaining what we are." We cannot become the man or woman we desire to become without growth. Your dreams need you to grow if it is going to grow. Remember, your dreams is ahead of you, not behind you. Your dreams are something that we aim toward. Other words for growth are advance, improvement, expansion, rise, success. Are you advancing on your dreams? Is there improvement? Because if there is none, then it's safe to assume that you are not growing.

Every day I read books and listen to inspirational videos that are related to my dreams. This allows me to grow. I first get the information, then I look for opportunities to apply the information. It is important that we study our craft because we only know what we study. Information is the blueprint to you reaching your dreams. When I am traveling to somewhere I have never been, I look to get the right information that is going to get me there. And I emphasize "the right information" because every road leads to somewhere, and the wrong information will lead you somewhere but not where you are trying to go.

I remember, when I was a young boy, my family would go on trips. Back in those days, we did not have GPS, so we relied on other people for directions. On many occasions, my family would be riding around in circles, lost and frustrated, simply because we were given the wrong information, we did not have the right information.

Your growth requires that you have the right information for you to get the desired results. I meet so many people who are frustrated with their life simply because they do not have the right information. When it comes to your dreams, do you have the right information? Because if not, you will not get where you are trying to go. And if you do have the right information, are you being *intentional* about applying it?

Joining the John C. Maxwell Team allowed me to get the right information, but applying the information was all on me. I had to be deliberate about applying the information.

It was up to me to read the material and apply it. It is up to you to apply the information that is in this book to help you grow. We all agreed that there is room in our life to grow and get better. But knowing is not enough. Knowing that I need to lose weight is not enough. I must do something with what I know. I must act on the information and make advancements to draw closer to the results that I want.

The more I read and study, the more I learn. The more I learn, the more I apply what I learn. The more I apply what I learn, the more results I see. Remember, growth is about becoming, becoming a better leader, provider, protector, man, or woman. Growth is about becoming a better you.

Is growth going to be easy? No, it is not. Growth is often painful but rewarding, if you stick with it. Growth hurts because you are being stretched. Growth requires us to come out of our comfort zones and often do things we have to do but not necessarily feel like doing. As I have gotten older, I do not enjoy working out like when I was younger. In my teens, I would hit the gym twice a day, but now once is a struggle.

But I understand without pain, there is no gain. I have learned to take my mind off the pain and focus my mind on the gain, the benefits, and the rewards that come because of my temporary pain. Focusing on the growth that is taking place keeps me motivated.

There will be things that you have to do but may not want to do. I must exercise daily if I want to get in shape and live a healthy life. I must read every day if I want to grow and become a better me.

It has been said, do what you have to do until you can do what you want to do. What are some things that you must do right now that are going to take you closer to your dreams? I wanted to buy a home, and for me to accomplish that, I had to establish my credit. I wanted to become a man of influence and value, so I had to become more valuable. So I took courses, went to seminars, and studied.

Make a list of the dreams that you have, and beside

them, write down what you must do to accomplish those dreams. The first thing you must do to grow and accomplish your dreams is get started. Most people fall short on their dreams because they fail to get started. It has been said, the journey to a thousand miles begins with one step. You cannot finish if you never get started.

Every book begins with one word. Every marathon begins with one step. Your dreams need you to take that first step. Step out of your comfort zone. Step out of the box of mediocrity. Before I was able to step into my greatness, I had to step out of my comfort zone. I had to step out of what was familiar. If everything around you look familiar, that means you have not gotten started yet. Remember, your dreams are what you are striving toward.

One of the joys I get from traveling is being in the unfamiliar, being able to enjoy different experiences outside of what I am used to. I enjoy the unfamiliar so much, I do not want to leave. Before my vacation ends, I am planning the next one. I am in search for the unfamiliar. Are you looking for the unfamiliar? Because that is where your dreams are. It has been said that if you want something new, then you must stop doing something old.

The other day, as I stepped out of my house, I ran into the unfamiliar. I noticed a large turtle slowly walking across my street, attempting to get to the other side. Now for me, this was unfamiliar. I grew up in the inner city of Baltimore. I was used to seeing cats, dogs, and even rats cross the street, but never in my life have I witnessed a turtle crossing the street.

I drew closer and observed the turtle. I even begin looking around, hoping to find someone I could share my new experience with. But no one was around. I then began to wonder, was this normal? Was this familiar to the new community I had moved into? And if so, I knew that I had grown, my life had changed, and I never wanted to go back to the familiar.

Observing the turtle was a teaching moment for me. To be honest, I thought about capturing the turtle. But this moment was to be captured and not the turtle. The turtle was not lost, it had a destination, and his destination was a pond on the side of my house. Even at a slow pace, the turtle was getting closer to his destination. Are you getting closer to your destination? It does not matter how slow you may be moving, but what matters is that you are moving in the right direction.

What also matters is your environment. In a different environment, this turtle would not have survived. He would have been captured and even killed. Do not allow your dreams to be captured or killed because you are in the wrong environment. Being around the wrong people can kill your dreams. Being in a relationship with the wrong person can kill your dreams. Also, being the wrong person can destroy your dreams. If who you are is not who you wish to become, then you must keep learning and keep growing because *we cannot become what we want by remaining what we are.*

I once heard it taught that there are five essential

factors for a growth environment, and I agree. A growth environment is a place where

1. Others are ahead of you. This allows you to see what you can become.

2. Others encourage you. Find friends who bring out the best in you.

3. You are out of your comfort zone. When was the last time you did something for the first time?

4. Failure is not your enemy. Growth allows you to "fail forward."

5. Others are growing. The journey together is most rewarding.

Now ask yourself based on those five essential factors for growth, am I in a growth environment? When you stay committed to growing yourself, at the end of the year, you will be able to say to others, "If you know me based on who I was a year ago, you don't know me at all. My growth game is strong. Allow me to reintroduce myself."

My friend, I look forward to meeting the new you. I look forward to you reintroducing yourself because your growth game is that strong.

Do not underestimate the importance of being in the right environment. Do not underestimate the importance of being in the right relationship. Do not underestimate the importance of being in the right church. Do not underestimate the importance of being around the right people. If you can answer yes to the above five essential factors, then you are in the right environment. If not, then you, my friend, have some tough decisions to make. Your dreams do matter, and so does the environment that you are in. Remember, *we cannot become what we want by remaining what we are*, and I'm going to add, *we cannot become what we want by remaining where we are*, and that is in the wrong environment.

Self Confidence

Always remember you are braver than you believe, stronger than you seem, and smarter than you think. —Christopher Robin

Wouldn't it be powerful if you fell in love with your dreams so deeply that you would do just about anything if you knew it would make you happy? This is how much your dreams love you and want you to nurture it. So my question is, what is stopping you? What is keeping you from falling in love with your dreams? What is stopping you from taking care of your dreams so in return your dreams can take care of you?

For many, the answer is a lack of self-confidence. You do not believe you are brave enough, strong enough, or smart enough. And because of lack of self-confidence, your dreams, your happiness, and your success are deferred. I remember, when I was about nine years old, I wanted to play Little League football. I went to the coach who happened to be my cousin through marriage. We were at my grandmother's house for the holiday. I walked up to him with confidence and said, "I want to play football for your team."

My cousin looked at me and smiled. I could tell from his expression that he was more amused than impressed. You see, stature never favored me. I was a short guy, but in my heart, I was a giant.

My cousin took me outside into the streets so he could give me a try out. He had me run to test my speed. I ran my little heart out. I felt like I was running for my life, and I was because as a kid, playing football was my dream. He then had someone throw to me as I ran routes. I caught every ball. A few weeks later, he invited me to the official tryouts. I was the youngest and smallest guy trying out.

And even though the coach was my cousin, he treated me the same, and I expected nothing less. I worked hard.

Many of the bigger players tried to intimidate me. They tried to rough me up, but I showed no fear and never gave up. When it was time to see who made the team, my name was on the list. And as time progressed, I did not just earn the other players' respect, but I also earned a starting position as a running back.

My dreams to play football on that level needed my confidence. And so does yours. Confidence is like commitment; without it, nothing happens.

So what is self-confidence? Self-confidence is a feeling of self-assurance arising from one's appreciations of one's own abilities or qualities. Or as Christopher Robin puts it, "It's remembering that you are braver than you believe, stronger than you seem, and smarter than you think." Self-confidence is extremely important in almost every aspect of our lives, yet so many people struggle to find it. And people who lack self-confidence can find it difficult to live out their dreams.

A lack of self-confidence is a self-sabotaging behavior and a dream killer to say the least. But the good news is that self-confidence can be learned and built on. And whether you are working on your own confidence or building the confidence of others around you, it is worth the effort. Your confidence in your dreams, or lack of, can show up in many ways: your behavior, your body language, how you speak, and what you say.

I remember, early in my career, I was given the opportunity to meet with some educators. I was trying to land their business, but instead, I landed flat on my face. As we sat around the table, they all stared at me as I made a fool out of myself. I lacked confidence, and it showed. I was stumbling over my words. I kept repeating myself, and I was sweating so hard, I thought I was going to pass out.

I ran out of that meeting so fast and felt bad for wasting their time. After a few days of having a pity party, I found the courage to confront myself. And what I discovered was my poor performance came because of poor preparation. I had forgotten the five Ps: proper preparation prevents poor performance. My lack of confidence came because of not preparing myself, which produced poor performance.

It has been said that champions don't become champions in the ring, it is only in the ring that they are recognized as champions. This is true, not only in sports, but also in life. Becoming a champion takes place outside of the ring. It is what you do to prepare for the fight that makes you a champion. It is what we do to prepare for success that makes us a champion. Once again, *proper preparation prevents poor performance.*

After that disaster of a meeting, I promised myself that I would never go into a situation without *proper preparation.* How is your preparation? Are you preparing yourself to live your dreams? What does your preparation look like and sound like? I mentioned earlier that without self-confidence, nothing happens. Building confidence should be part of your preparation, if you expect something to happen. What does your self-talk sound like? Do you doubt your abilities to succeed? Do you always find excuses to not try?

Do you remember the story "The Little Engine That Could"? What a great story for children to build self-confidence! The little engine was confronted with a big task. He was challenged to do something he never did before. And with a little encouragement, the little engine agreed to take on a task that all others refused. Starting out, the little engine's dialogue went like this: "I think I can, I think I can, I think I can."

And as the little engine gained momentum, his self-confidence changed, and so did his inner dialogue. He went from "I think I can" to "I know I can."

Do you think you can live your dreams? Do you think you can be successful? Do you think you can be happy? Do you think you can have a good quality of life, or do you know you can? If you have not come to the point of knowing that you can, then something must change. And that something is you because nothing changes until we change. You will continue to treat yourself the way that you see yourself. If you think you cannot, then you will not.

Building self-confidence is necessary if you are to live your dreams. And the good news is that it is achievable. So here are three steps to self-confidence: preparing for the journey, setting out, and accelerating toward success.

Step 1: Preparing for the Journey

The first step involves getting ready for your journey to self-confidence. It is important to think about where you are, think about where you want to go, get yourself in the right mindset for your journey, and commit yourself to starting it and staying with it. As you can see, many of these steps were covered in previous chapters.

In preparing for your journey to build confidence, the first thing you want to do is look at what you already achieved. Reflect on your life and write down some things that you have already accomplished. It does not matter how insignificant you may think it was. The fact is you accomplished it.

As I write this book, I have two of my books that I published in front of me as a reminder that *I know I can, I know I can*. Enjoy your past success as it reminds you that you can accomplish anything you put your mind to.

The second thing you must do is think about your strengths. What are you passionate about? What you are good at? Truth is, nobody starts off good, but everyone starts off with passion. Your passion to achieve success and live your dreams is a strength. Your passion to help people and influence people is a strength. It's been said, you find your passion, you find your purpose. And in most cases, others will see it before you do. Before I thought about writing a book, I used to enjoy writing short stories and poetry. One day my friend Sharonda was reading what I had written and asked me if I ever thought about writing a book. Until Sharonda suggested I write a book, I had never considered it. Sharonda was able to see what I could not.

I thought about it, and my thoughts went from "I think I can" to "I know I can." And guess what, I did write that book. And now I am working on publishing my third book.

You see, my passion for writing led to my purpose to help people, encourage people, and minister to people. Did I start off good? No, I did not, but I did get started. It was the same for me when I played football. I started off on the bench. The coach would put me in during the kickoff, and that was it. But I stuck with it, not because I was good, but because I was passionate. My passion for the game was my strength, and that was enough to keep me from quitting. Your passion will buy you time, the time you need to get better, stronger, and build on your confidence.

The third thing is think about what's important to you and where you want to go. Achieving your dreams should be important to you. And if it were not, you would not be reading this book. Remember, it is your dream, and if it is not important to you, then do not expect it to be important to anyone else. And how can you tell if your dreams are important? Well, just look at the attention you give it. Are you feeding your dreams or starving it? Do you invest in your dreams? Are you giving it the things that it needs from you?

Your dreams must be important to you if it is going to survive. Yes, I said "survive" because dreams do die when abandoned. From a scale of 1 to 10, and 10 being the greatest of importance, how would you rate the level of importance of your dreams? If you say your level of importance is anything less than a 10, then your dreams could potentially die. Nothing should be more important than you achieving your dreams. Your dreams are tied to your purpose, and if you have no purpose, you will have no destination.

Every time I lose focus of my purpose, I lose myself. I do not have a clear direction without purpose. Our dreams are our life blueprint. Our dreams serve as a pattern, a guide, to assure that we are living our life with purpose. Your dreams tell you where you want to go. There is a blueprint in your mind that will lead you to happiness, peace, blessings, only if you are willing to follow it.

The blueprint in your mind needs to be written down on paper. It is called goal setting. Goal setting is the process you use to set targets for yourself and measure your success of hitting those targets.

Step 2: Stepping Out

This is where you start moving toward your goals. By doing the right things and starting small, you will put yourself on the path to success and start building the self-confidence that comes with it. I shared with you that before I wrote my first book, I started writing poems and short stories. These were small steps toward greater accomplishments.

The same principle applied to my speaking career. My first speaking engagement was to a summer camp of about ten to fifteen elementary- and middle school-age students. When I got the invitation, I prepared like I was speaking to corporate America. I spoke with passion and did not hold back. I felt like the coach was taking me off the bench and putting me in the game. This was my time to build my confidence. It has been said, never underestimate small beginnings. On whatever level you may be on, take yourself seriously. Take your gifts seriously because your gifts are said *to make room for you and bring you before great men.*

What I mean by taking yourself seriously is build the knowledge you need to succeed. When I begin to understand where I wanted to go based on my life blueprint, I started gathering the tools I needed to get there. I joined an organization that is number one in the world in terms of leadership development, the John Maxwell Team. I wanted to be my best, so I joined the best. The John Maxwell Team has given me the tools to be effective in my craft. Having a strong desire was enough to get me started, but it was not enough to make me affective. I needed resources, I needed more to become more.

To be your best, you must give your best. The more

you have, the more you must give. So you must invest in your dreams. You must sharpen your tools. Wherever your dreams are leading you, find people who are already living the dream and follow their lead. For good leaders are great followers.

Who are you following? Take a page from their book. There are people like Les Brown, Zig Ziglar, Tony Robins, John C. Maxwell, T. D. Jakes, and many more who have become my mentors. I do not have direct access to these great men, but I connect with them through their books and videos. I read what they read and allow them to pour into my life.

Another thing that is important to stepping out is to keep managing your mind. Managing your mind is no different from managing your money. You mismanage your money, you will lose it, the same with your mind. A sure way to lose your mind is to allow it to run wild and have no direction. You manage your mind through discipline and what I call pause moments. A pause moment is a planned time you set aside to evaluate your life. It is a moment to reflect and to adjust if necessary. And yes, it will be necessary because the greatest challenge to any success is staying on course.

One of the ways I manage my mind is by reading and listening to sermons and positive speeches. This gets me going in the right direction and helps me stay on course. As James Allen's book puts it, "As a man thinkenth," and the Bible adds, "So is he." We become what we think. So what are you thinking every day, all day? I am always thinking about the next level, the next project. I am always thinking about the good things that God has in store for me.

I am managing my mind to keep from losing my mind. Another way to manage your mind is to invest in your mind. Attend seminars and workshops. Purchase books and hire a coach who can come alongside you to assist you on the most important journey of your life.

If your dreams are not important enough for you to invest your time and money, then chances are your dreams will die because of neglect. Do not abort your dreams, give your dreams what it needs, and it will give you what you need.

Step 3: Accelerating Toward Success

At this stage, you will feel self-confidence building. You would have, by this time, completed some trainings, managed your mind, and established some discipline. Now it is time to stretch yourself. Make your goals a bit bigger and challenges a bit tougher.

This is my first leadership development personal growth book. I am stretching myself. I have wrestled with the thought of writing such a book for quite some time. I had the "I think I can, I think I can" mindset, which means I doubted myself. I had good intentions but was not intentional. I lacked confidence to go to the next level. So I started looking back at what I had already accomplished, and I realized something. I realized I always begin with "I think I can." And "I think I can" was better than saying "I know I can't."

Then the light came on when I began to think about what my dreams needed from me. And the first thing that came to mind was *my commitment*, and without commitment, nothing happens. When I decided to commit myself, I went from "I think I can, I think I can" to "I know I can, I know I can." You are reading this book because I build on my self-confidence.

I am still the little engine that could, and so are you. You can accomplish your dreams if you know you can. You can rewrite your story if you know you can. You can start your own business if you know you can. Repeat these words: "When it comes to my dreams, I know I can, I know I can."

CHOICES

In order to make changes, you must make choices. —Herbert Fenner

My purpose for writing this book is to bring about change. But I have come to realize that without making choices, there will be no change. The late Jim Rohn once said, "If you want things to change, you have to change." And if you are going to change, you must be willing to make a choice to change.

When I was a teenager, I made some poor choices. Choices that landed me in federal prison. I made choices that caused me and those close to me pain. While in prison, I had time to reflect on my life and the choices that placed me there. I was young and naïve, but it did not take long for me to know that I wanted change. I was in an obscure place, and I had an ugly problem, and my problem was I did not know who I was.

I had no identity apart from what people had said about me. And if it is true that we are a sum of the choices we make, that meant that I was not much at all. I was a failure to say the least. What about you? What do your choices say about you? And regardless of what it says, if you do not like what it says, then you, my friend, can change it. That is the beauty in choices: It brings about changes.

My life was not over, and neither is yours. And the greatest revelation that I could ever receive was that I could rewrite my story. I had the opportunity to change characters and switch roles. If I wanted something different, I had to be willing to become something different. I had a choice, and I chose to become the man I am today.

Michael Jackson had a song that said, "I'm looking at the man in the mirror, and I'm asking him to change his ways." Are you satisfied with the man or woman you see in the mirror? Are you happy and content with that person you see? If not, then ask him or her to change his or her ways. Ask him or her to do better to get better. And remind him or her that "if you want things to change, then you have to change."

Making the right choices is something that your dreams need from you. Everything that has been covered in this book so far requires a choice: commitment, vision, faith, growth, self-confidence. For without choices, there will be no changes.

One of the things that helps me make choices is knowing the benefits of the choices. And I want to talk about some of the benefits that come with choices. Now what is a benefit? A benefit is described as something that is advantageous, something good. I do not know about you, but this works for me: Making a choice can bring about something good. Yes, it can. The benefits of choices: you have freedom, you are in control of your life, you have the ability to make your life better, you have the possibility to reach your potential, you can change the direction of your life. If you noticed, each benefit began with *you*. This is a choice you must make. This is where you take your life back and accept responsibility for your choices.

Earlier, I stated that if you do not like who you see in the mirror, then change who you see in the mirror because I did. Choices give you freedom. A slave was a slave because of their lack of freedom. And you do not have to be a slave physically, although you can be a slave mentally. A mental slave is a person who refuses to make different choices and continues to get the same results.

There was this story about a man who, as he was passing by some elephants, suddenly stopped, confused by the fact that these huge creatures were being held by only a small rope tied to their front leg. No chains, no cages. It was obvious that the elephant could at any time break away from their bonds, but for some reason, they did not.

The man saw a trainer nearby and asked why these animals just stood there and make no attempt to get away.

"Well," the trainer said, "when they are young and much smaller, we use the same size ropes to tie them, and at that age, it's enough to hold them. As they grow up, they are conditioned to believe the rope can still hold them, so they never try to break free."

Like the elephants, how many of us go through life with these limited beliefs about ourselves? You judge your future by what happened in your past. We think to ourselves, "I tried that before, and it did not work out, so why bother trying again?" "Well, they said I cannot do it, so why should I waste my time?"

They said Michael Jordan was not good enough in high school, but Michael Jordan chose to think different. Did you forget that the benefits of choices start with you? What they say is not important. It is what you say about you that matters. It is what you say about your dreams that matters. If you want to be free from limiting beliefs about who you are and what you can accomplish, then make a choice today. Choose to be free.

Choices give you control over your life. If you do not like what you see, then change it. There was a story I heard about people visiting a wise man complaining about the same problem repeatedly. One day he decided to tell them a joke, and they all roared with laughter. After a few minutes, he told them the same joke, and only a few smiled. Then he told the same joke for a third time, but no one laughed or smiled anymore. The wise man smiled and said, "You can't laugh at the same joke over and over. So why are you always crying about the same problem?"

Choices give you control over your life. When I understood that I could control my day by the choices I make, I decided to be conscious of my choices. You do not have to complain; you chose to. You do not have to be broke; you chose to. You do not have to be in a relationship you are not valued; you chose to. Take your control back by choosing to not complain, not give up, and not quit.

Another benefit is the ability to make your life better. If you are reading this book, it's because you believe that your dreams matter and you want to make your life better. I like to say "rewrite your story." When you look at where you are at right now, are you happy? Or do you feel like something is missing? Are you okay with the character and role you are playing in your story, or do you feel like you need to switch roles?

I always say that every road will lead to somewhere. So my question is, where are you headed? As a teenager, the role I played in my story was headed to prison or to an early grave. I didn't like where I was going, so I had to change my character to change my destination. I started making choices that would make my life better. I chose to go back to school to get my GED. Then I chose to enroll in college to get my degree. I chose to give my life to God and allow God to use me to bring people to salvation. I chose to make new friends. And with every new choice came change.

My life got better because I got better. And if you expect your life to get better, then you must get better. You must make better choices, and remember, a better life will be the benefit that you will receive, a life that is worth living, a life with meaning and purpose, a life full of joy and happiness. You can live a life that says, "My dreams matter."

Another great benefit is the possibility to reach your potential. Yes, there is still much to discover about you. You have unlimited potential, but like most people, you are in the wrong environment. And yes, your environment does matter. I discovered the importance of being in the right environment when I read this story about this archeologist. The archeologist had discovered this ancient tomb that belonged to one of the pharaohs. Inside the tomb was ancient artifacts, such as silver, gold, and statues. Also, among the artifacts were some corn seeds. The archeologist was curious and wanted to know if the corn seeds had the potential to grow, considering that it had been buried in a tomb for thousands of years. The archeologist took the corn seeds and planted it by the Nile river. And within weeks, the seeds began to grow and produce corn. The archeologist discovered that there was nothing wrong with the corn seeds, it had unlimited potential, but it was buried in the wrong environment.

Like the corn seeds, you have unlimited potential, but you cannot grow because of your environment. You are hanging out with the wrong people. It has been said that if you hang around nine broke people, chances are you will be number ten. If you hang around nine depressed people, chances are you will be number ten. The same principle applies to hanging around nine wealthy people. Chances are you will be number ten. Birds of a feather do flock together. Eagles do not hang with ducks. Are you going to soar with the eagles or quack with the ducks? You have a choice, and as for me, I chose to soar with the eagles. I chose to associate with people who can bring out the best in me and not the worse. So remember, when it comes to your dreams, your environment matters.

The last benefit for me is one benefit that makes making choices all worth it, and that is you can change the direction of your life. It has been said that you can't change your destiny over night, but you can change your direction overnight.

It may take years to reach your destiny, but it only takes a choice to change your direction. When you look at your life right now, what direction are you headed in? And the way to tell is by the choices that you are making. When I was young, I did not understand why or how people could predict my future. They would say things like "you are going to end up in prison or dead." I hated to hear those things, and I argued against it. But they were right. These people were not hating on me as I thought. They were simply telling my future by evaluating my choices. And when my choices changed, their evaluation changed.

How do you predict your future? What do you see yourself doing five years from now? What kind of life do you want to live and legacy to leave? These questions are important, and knowing what you want will help in determining the choices you have to make. If I was planting a garden, knowing what I want in my garden will determine the type of seeds I have to plant. If I want a rose garden, I would plant rose seeds.

If you want financial prosperity, then you must make choices that is going to produce that. If you want peace, then you must make choices that will produce that. Not only do you have to make the right choice, but you also have to protect your choice. There will be people who will oppose your choice, and if you do not protect it, you will not reap the benefits of that choice.

I remember an old friend reached out to me with some confusion, but he was not aware that I made a choice to have peace. So to protect my choice to have peace, I blocked him from contacting me. I had to protect my choice, so I made another choice. Remember, to make changes, we must make choices.

If you do not like the direction your career is headed, it is not too late to change directions. If you do not like the direction your business is headed, it is not too late to change directions. If you do not like the direction your life is headed, it is not too late to change directions. This is the power behind your choice. One choice can change the trajectory of your life. Your life will change the moment you make a choice to change it.

A Pause Moment

Practice the pause. When in doubt, pause.

When angry, pause. When tired, pause. When

stressed, pause. And when you pause, pray.

I was introduced to the "pause moment" by my mentor and coach Dr. John C. Maxwell in his book *The 15 Invaluable Laws of Growth*. Dr. Maxwell stated that "if someone is going down the wrong road, he doesn't need motivation to speed up. He needs to stop." Out of the many principles that I teach people who are looking to grow their business and to grow themselves, the pause moment is one that I emphasize the most. I find the pause moment to be a critical principle to follow and tool to use. A pause moment is a moment of reflection, a moment of evaluation, and a moment of self-discovery.

Had I been introduced to the pause moment earlier in my life, I am certain many of the detours in my life could have been prevented. So to avoid further detours, I've implemented the pause moment to my life. A pause moment is like giving yourself a weekly checkup, a weekly examination. A pause moment is a moment to stop all activity and all movement to reflect and, if necessary, make adjustment. And yes, adjustments will be necessary. Thomas Merton once said, "People may spend their whole lives climbing the ladder of success only to find, once they reach the top, that the ladder is leaning against the wrong wall."

Is your ladder leaning against the wrong wall? Have you been investing your time and energy in the wrong relationship because you feel obligated to commit yourself because of low or no self-esteem? Have you been given your best years to the wrong company, a company that does not appreciate you, and every time you get paid, it shows? Did you go to school and get the wrong degree because at the time it was something everyone else was pursuing, but you really do not have any passion in that area? If you have answered yes to any of these, then it is time to have a pause moment.

The first pause moment that I ever encountered was not intentional. I was not planning to have one, I was forced to have one. And even though this pause moment was affective, it's not the type of pause moment that I would recommend you wait for. I was being detained in a federal holdover facility hundreds of miles away from home. At this point in my life, I was so lost, I could not tell you which way was up. I remember it just like it was yesterday, and it's been over twenty-five years ago. I was sitting in a holding cell, isolated with no one else to talk to but myself. I was having a pause moment, a moment to reflect on my life and the choices that I had made to put myself in that situation. I was forced to look at the man in the mirror, and it pained me because I did not recognize the man I saw. Over the years of making bad choices and succumbing to negative peer pressure, I had become unrecognizable. My ladder of success was leaning against the wrong wall. It was leaning against a wall with barbed wires and shotgun towers. Tears began to stream down my face because I really did not know how I had gotten there. I did not know how I had become the person that I had become.

In hindsight, I realize that if I had only taken the time to pause and reflect on my life and the decisions I was making, I would have recognized that my ladder was against the wrong wall. Do not wait until you reach the top of your ladder before you realize that it is against the wrong wall. Do not wait until your freedom is on the line before you realize you are against the wrong wall. Do not wait until you are too old before you realize your ladder is against the wrong wall. Do not wait until you are burned out until you realize you are investing in the wrong business. Do not wait until you have no more love to give before you realize you are in the wrong relationship. Do not wait until it is too late before you realize that your dreams matter.

Your dreams matter, and if you are going to be successful at reaching the top of your ladder, you will need to have a pause moment. You will need to *"practice the pause. When in doubt, pause. When angry, pause. When tired, pause. When stressed, pause. And when you pause, pray.*

Practicing the pause moment is critical to you achieving your dreams. To practice the pause moment, you must be intentional about setting aside time each week, and in some cases each day, to reflect on the choices you are making and how those choices are affecting you and your success. Practicing the pause moment must become part of your regimen. When you take a moment to pause, remember this is the time to be honest with your assessment. This is the time to examine your thinking and your actions that follow. This is the time to pinpoint your exact location as it pertains to your dreams and the life you desire to live. This is not the time to have a pity party or woe-is-me party.

This is not the time to make excuses, but this is the time to adjust.

When in doubt, pause. There will be times when you will doubt the decisions you have made and the ones that you need to make. Some choices that we must make are not always clear, especially when we are being controlled by our emotions. Some choices that we must make may not be clear when you do not have all the right information. The pause moment is a safeguard to your success. When in doubt, pause. Life is full of crossroads, and from the time you wake up, you will have to make choices. Some choices will come easy, but others will be complicated. When I find myself in doubt, I have learned to just sit still and do nothing until I reevaluate my thinking and where my choices will lead me. It has been said that prevention is better than cure, and I agree. Do not allow anyone to push you to make a choice that you are not comfortable with making because at the end of the day, you will be the one left with the consequences.

When angry, pause. As you pursue your dreams, you will have moments of frustration, and there will be times when you will become angry. You will get angry or frustrated at the process of achieving your dreams. Yes, to achieve your dreams, you must go through a growth process. And I must admit it can be painful. We heard it said that without pain, there is no gain. Pain, in some cases, is the prerequisite to change. When you look at history, many of the changes that has come about came because of people getting angry at their life, their circumstances, and then being angry enough to do something about it. Being angry is not a bad thing, especially when your anger is used as your motivator to push you to act and bring about change. When I had my first pause moment in prison, I was angry. I was angry at the choices that I had made and where they had landed me. I was so angry that I decided to use my anger to not become bitter but to become better. I did not use my anger to point fingers and play the blame game. I accepted responsibility for my choices and used my anger to rewrite my story.

Anger does not have to be your enemy. Whatever is making you angry, you have the power to change it. And if you cannot change your situation, you can change the way that you look at it. I could not change my situation in prison, so I decided to change how I looked at my situation in prison. For some, prison was the school of hard knocks, but for me, prison was a place to rewrite my story. I have learned that *nothing changes until we change*. So if you are in a situation that you do not like, and this situation is making you angry, then I would encourage you to do something about it. I would encourage you to change, and your situation will change. My anger brought about my change and helped me become the man I am today.

When tired, pause. One of my favorite scriptures says that "The race is not given to the swift nor to the strong," Ecclesiastes 9:11-12. And in many cases, the part that says, "To those that endures until the end" is something we added. But nonetheless, the point is accurate. Pursuing your dreams is not a sprint run. Your dreams are going to take time to cultivate. Your dreams are not about the destination as much as it is about the journey that leads to the destination. To accomplish your dreams, you are going to need endurance. Every so often you are required to take a break. When we get tired, it reflects in our work and in the choices we make. You ever heard it said that the worse time to go grocery shopping is when you are hungry. It's true because you end up buying things that you do not need. Working when you are tired can be detrimental to your growth, so to avoid needing a cure, let's just work on prevention. Sometimes, when I am writing, I get tired and must take a break. This break allows me to get the needed rest and come back with fresh eyes.

Even God took a break from his work with creation. God took a pause moment and rested on the seventh day to reflect on what he had created. To avoid burn out, you must take a pause moment. Work then rest, work then rest. And resting does not mean working, resting means resting. When I am restless, I am irritated and frustrated to say the least. But when I take the time to lay my work down and get rest, I find myself more affective with my work. I find myself more creative. The worse time to make critical decisions is when you are tired. And when I say tired, I am talking mentally and physically. Your dreams are too important to make decisions when you are not fully rested. A lack of rest will be the cause of your reaching the top of the ladder of success and then realizing that your ladder is against the wrong wall.

When stressed, pause. One of the leading causes of stress is a lack of rest. As much as you may think that you are like the Energizer bunny, and you can keep going and going and going, I must be the bearer of bad news: You will not last. Stress will kill you, if you do not learn to pause and rest. Not only will stress kill you, but people will also kill you if you allow them to. Early on in my ministry and coaching career, I would be under a tremendous amount of stress because of a lack of rest. I felt like I was obligated to answer every call and that it was my duty to help everybody who I felt needed it. The sooner I realized that my gifts does not make me a god, I was able to say no. Learning how to say no will add years to your life. When it comes to your dreams, you cannot be a yes-man. A yes-man soon becomes a dead man.

Too many yeses lead to stress. My pastor and friend, the late Pastor Leroy Sullivan, sat me down in my early years of ministry. He told me that many people will recognize the gifts and calling that God has placed on my life and many will attempt to use me for their own personal reasons. He said that he would not allow that to happen, and there will be times when I would have to say no. After Pastor Sullivan had transitioned to be with the Lord, his words came true. I was being pulled in many different directions. But at the time, I felt like I was being recognized for the call on my life. I was under a lot of stress because I realized I was being used to further someone else's cause. I found myself under stress because people who I had assisted did not appreciate me, only what I could do for them.

Be careful when it comes to your dreams and the gifts that God has given you. People will not want you but what you have to offer. They will not speak to you nor call you until they need something from you. And this can lead to stress. When you find yourself under stress, take a moment to reflect on what is going on in your life and make adjustments. Stress is not your friend; it is an enemy to your dreams. At the first sign of stress, pause.

And when you pause, pray. Remember, a pause moment is a time to reflect, evaluate, and discover. And most of these will take place when you pray. Prayer is a method of communicating with God, the one who holds your future. God says, "I know the plans that I have for you, plans to prosper you and not harm you, plans to give you hope and a future."

When I had my first unintentional pause moment in prison, it was prayer that got me on course and headed me in the right direction. At the time, I was lost, and my life did not have any meaning. It was not until I asked God who I was that my life began to change. I did not know that God had good thoughts toward me and a plan to give me hope and a future. I asked a question, and God had the answer. Everything that I have become that is good is a result of the purpose and plan God had for me and not so much the plans I had for myself.

If you have come to the end of this book but not the end of your life, and you are still uncertain about your dreams and your life purpose, then I would encourage you to pause and pray. Prayer changes things as you can see from my personal testimonies. Just ask God who you are and what his plans for your life are. He will show you who you are and the plans he has for you. I cannot tell you what those plans are, but I can tell you that God's plans for you is not to harm you but to give you hope and a future. Yes, it's not too late to have a bright future. It's not too late to live your dreams because your dreams do matter.

CPSIA information can be obtained
at www.ICGtesting.com
Printed in the USA
LVHW041008080621
689682LV00005B/184

9 781664 176720